TEARS OF
ASH AND LIGHT

PURPLE PHOENIX POETRY

Tears of Ash and Light

ISBN: 978-1-7775476-2-2

for A

thank you for showing me the light while I was still
in ashes

CONTENTS

i write to share hope & light in the darkness, and the
images and words in this book reflect this dream

this is a story of rising to *become*

i hope that you see pieces of your beautiful soul within the
light,
too

keep shining

Come, dream with me

FIRE

FIRE

her words drip like poison onto the page

a raw,
bloody,
broken,
mess

held in flawless pages

FIRE

you were a talented arsonist,
creating a brilliant fire

you told me you loved me
even as you burned the life from my lungs

FIRE

you broke me

and now i'm supposed to trust again?

FIRE

the mask kept slipping
in your masquerade ball
until i couldn't find
prince charming

there was only a beast

and me,
a broken girl who once believed she was a princess

FIRE

she condemns her tears to a silent death

it
does
not
matter

and you
will
not
care

sometimes the only way to survive
is to lie to the broken parts of herself

FIRE

it took a certain kind of hell
to break the unbreakable
that lived
within her soul

her thoughts are a prison
and she has been given a life sentence

i fell in love with who i wanted you to be

— imaginary

FIRE

i became lost in your ocean
craving an anchor to ground me in the waves
of my own mind

you stirred the storm
while promising me land

- *and now you are sailing away*

it is breaking my heart
to break yours
i want to scream
and cry
and hold you so tightly
that the fantasy of us
working out
could be reality

i am drowning
and i am pushing away
the only person
i want to save me

- *but i must*

FIRE

i could cry a million tears
and it still wouldn't make you

stay

FIRE

you keep my heart in a cage
and bring spectators to parade by

for a price, of course

it is a wild thing,
this heart,
so bloodied and scarred

the wildness enchants viewers

but the wildness never allures you
the only you thing you crave
is the fame
my dissected heart brings

it is only a tool,
a means to an end
and you have made me
the fool

FIRE

memories haunt her (1)

scared
don't make me

they laugh
they pressure

she swims,
terrified

sharks

not in lakes,
but in her mind

she climbs in the boat
and they congratulate her bravery

she smiles,
teeth chattering
as she pretends their insistence
didn't panic her little girl self

the boat begins the long way home
and she acts like it's okay

they laugh and talk and joke and shiver
in the cool air

she thinks and fears and puts on the mask that's gotten
her through this before
she's feisty
but the desire to belong
to be accepted
won this time

FIRE

the boat glides over the lake
as she stares at the churning surf
that she imagines hides so much

murky surface
needing to belong

she huddles and smiles and puts on the cloak of false
confidence

maybe tomorrow she'll be strong

she pleaded for him to call,
then kept her phone by her side,
waiting
for the words in the call
that would fix the shattered pieces of her heart

-   *it never came*

FIRE

i read about you in a book
every behavior
and hateful word
written in stark ink

you are the classic example
of everything i was taught to avoid

so why do i still love you?

FIRE

your words twist around me like worms
biting my flesh
while your hands cover me with flowers

you bandage my wounds
with a touch like silk
even as i beg for clarity
in your cloud of infected confusion

you smile with a mouthful of vengeance
holding my arm with such gentleness
as i choke on the poison emanating from your tongue

i whisper of my need to know
but you tell me that i am too stupid
to understand

FIRE

i am too broken
to take anyone's words
at face value

- *please understand*

FIRE

i learned to love a monster
by loving a man

i didn't fall for your dismissive cruelty;
i fell for who i was trying to get back

that beautiful and kind enigma
that you presented
at all the right times

FIRE

the loudest sound isn't a heart breaking

rather,

it's the sound of a heart pretending not to

sometimes it feels like we are a memory game,
aimlessly flipping tiles until our hearts match

\-   *i don't want to play anymore*

FIRE

all i ever wanted to do was stay afloat
and
make you love me

now i'm here

alone

and

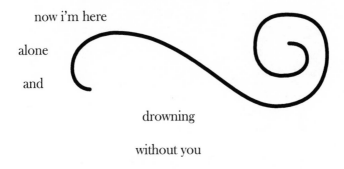

drowning

without you

FIRE

there are so many things wrong
but i ignore them all
because i want you to be right

- *for me*

i hold the jagged edges of the world
in my bloodied and broken hands

FIRE

another traumatic event

remembering,
she refuses to think

if she thinks,
her heart will break

and a broken heart never saved her

FIRE

just another girl trying to figure out
how to ignore her way
into goodbye

FIRE

you tell me it is my fault

that i created the monster you became

you made my wounds
and filled them with salt

now all i have left
is shame

she finds herself in the broken pieces

of an imaginary life

FIRE

maybe you'll forget me someday

but

try as i might

i can't forget how to breathe

FIRE

you said i was **different**

but you were the same as all the rest

FIRE

she sees him again, one year later
and suddenly she is on one side of a canyon,
her other, logical side yelling across

don't fall in
don't fall for him again

far down below she can
see him,
but she can't tell if he's
beckoning to her
or waving her away

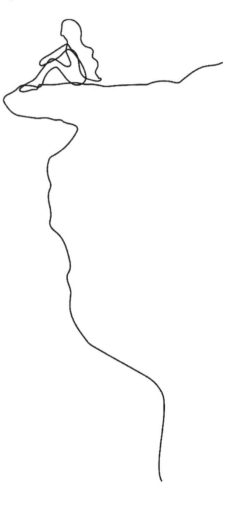

the part of her that fell
before wants to jump
but she knows:
there would only be
pain at the end

logic is screaming at her
to stay back
to step away from the
cliff-edge

but she keeps seeing
him,
within reach
if she just
stepped
off

she edges closer,
prepares to jump,
then sees him walk away

he doesn't look back,
and logic whispers farewell

FIRE

you crafted your lies

until i called them truth

just so you would stay

FIRE

she wonders why love became chains

maybe she didn't love hard enough?

or was it only that her soul was never allowed to be free?

FIRE

i was the moon,
guiding your way home through the darkness

you were the sun,
forever eclipsing me with your brilliance

FIRE

she copes by imagining herself somewhere this pain
never was

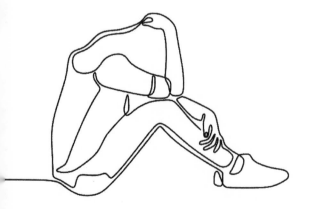

FIRE

sorrow drips like blood
from her hands

she cannot hold
this weight any longer

-   *it is breaking her*

FIRE

how long can a heart keep surviving until there's nothing
left to push away?

FIRE

he promised her heaven
but then he created hell

FIRE

there are words within her

some scream to be released
and some bloom with the most delicate of blood-stained
petals

she silences them

for she knows the danger that comes
with having a voice

FIRE

i crave romanticizing this madness
but logic says the beast didn't become gentle
because she loved him
just
enough

FIRE

she is excavating her heart,
searching for something
that will love
despite his words

FIRE

you promised me your everything,
swore your heart into my hand

the only thing you wouldn't give me
was honesty

FIRE

you were my first heart
                    b
                    r
                    e
                    a
                    k

you should really get a medal

-    *my heart was never easy to break*

FIRE

you lit my soul on fire with your professions of love

*i sparkled for you
and you alone*

it took so long for me to realize
that you created fires
simply because you loved
to watch them burn

- *gaslighter*

FIRE

you were my dream-turned-nightmare

you broke me

and still...

i love you

she talks to him about the past so much

remember how we met?
what we said?
what we did?

revisiting the past
dulls the pain of the present

for surely those moments are still there

if she just tries hard enough
she can get them back

if only the beauty
of those first moments
had lasted

but,
perhaps
they only existed
in her imagination

remembering the past
keeps her chained
in the present

FIRE

your fingers are stained with the murder of my dreams

-    *blood guilt*

FIRE

loving you,
trusting you would never leave,
was a sweet poison
to me

i died with the taste of your name
on my lips

FIRE

i gave you the knife
trusting you not to use it

i let down my guard
hoping you'd stay

i gave you my heart
believing you wouldn't break it

and then
you left

FIRE

i hold your love with shaking hands
always afraid i'll drop it
say the wrong thing
and you'll sit up in these hands of mine
stretch
and walk

     away

FIRE

sometimes loving you fits into my life like an old friend
and sometimes
it feels like i am dragging an anvil
by my fingernail

FIRE

our love died with the setting sun,

soaked in the dying embers

of another day

FIRE

i became the sun
orbiting your world

you craved my light
to illuminate your darkness

they wanted sunlight
and you could not give it

i shone for you,
believing that one day,
you would shine for me too

i should have recognized the night in your soul

FIRE

your love was like a dagger
wrapped in roses

the petals held the pain
until it was buried in my chest

-     *flowers from blood*

FIRE

when i stayed up late into the night,
desperately reading about how to know
if someone was lying,

i knew:
it had gone too far

FIRE

she needs

to learn to pour water over

her heart in the frozen air

so that it cannot

feel

FIRE

gaslighting

i loved you like a siren
singing my song

i never meant to lure you in
you said you walked in with eyes wide open

i believed you would hold my broken heart
like you promised to

i believed in *you*

after all,
why would you lie?

we lasted for so long,
each completely in love with the mirage in front of us

i hid my pain,
and you twisted yours until it was unrecognizable

then,
i made a fatal error:
i became more real

as i tiptoed into trusting you more,
i began to let my guard fall
my guard fell fast, and hard
as fast as i fell for you

i gave you pieces of my heart
that i had reserved only for me

i threw away the *off limits* sign
and handed you the key to a haunted past

FIRE

but you were brave,
and i knew i could trust you in that darkened house

i held your hand
as we walked through the shattered pieces
you carried me so that i wouldn't cut my feet on the glass

i trusted you

i knew that i was a mess
after all,
you reminded me every day
as you kissed the pieces that you said
made your heart bleed

but i guess i wanted to be loved a little too much
i wanted you to love all of me
and all of me was a lot

you began to twist my own words around my neck,
choking me with my phrases
that you used to say were so sweet

you used my love to squeeze the life from my lungs

when i asked about your game
you lit a match to illuminate your face
i saw the face of the man i loved so well
but the mask melted away
and i saw you as you really were

you dropped the match,
and i went up in flames

the last thing i saw
before i burned alive
was a stranger's face

FIRE

he pushed her away
until he realized:

she was already gone

A
S
H

ASH

the stain of another man's sin
paints her world grey

ASH

sometimes he was kind

sometimes he was gentle

sometimes he was loving

those were the moments she clung to

but now,

she is learning that she cannot survive on

sometimes

ASH

armor – part I

the sun glints off the silver

chainmail made with strong hands,
a scabbard with a sword,
a helmet hiding her eyes

ready to defend

but please
just look at me
see that i am still here

just a girl with armor

my shield is strong
the walls around my shattered heart are unbreakable
no weapon can pierce my silver skin
no eyes will see beyond

but please

just look at me
see that i am still here

just a girl with armor

ASH

i invested in you
with everything i had

you were the collateral of my life

without warning,
you evicted me from your heart

it's cold out here

ASH

if i had known it was the last time i would see you
would i have done any differently?

  -    *say something*

ASH

she embraces sorrow
despite her lifelong fear of it

ASH

i loved to fly

but you grabbed my hand
as you laughed and said:

come down to earth
you need to land

ASH

you thought i wouldn't see your game
as you looked into my eyes
and lied with a smile full of false promises

but you forgot:
i have lived this life before
studied each step in this game
and i am a master
at discovering
who is playing

ASH

i remember thinking
after your outburst

that i would never date someone like you

except that i knew you

now i realize:
i never knew you at all

ASH

part I

all that remains of us
is a pile of old photographs

i wonder if our colorful smiles were real
or if,
even then,
we realized that we were fading to grey

perhaps even in the magic of the beginning
we could see through the camera lens
to the ending

part II

the only place i see your face anymore
is in aged photos
i miss the shell of a man
reflected in the glossy prints

do you miss me too?

ASH

she finds safety in walking solo
here she is comfortable

yet

it is hard

to be alone

again

ASH

her tears never seem to end
burning her with fire
and leaving ash
where there was once life

she longs for the rebirth
that will signal the end
of this slow agony

they say it will take years
to reach healing

she longs
to be free
to dance
again

ASH

we were dizzy planets
colliding in the cosmos of a universe
called Love

it was a beautiful dance,
but eventually,
all collisions

      b

         r

            e

               a

                  k

                       -   *our galaxy*

ASH

you retreated to a world
where you say i cannot follow

i used to know your thoughts
your dreams
your passions

and now i am here
alone
without your mind or your arms
around me

-    *i miss you*

ASH

you created an elaborate game
and invited me to play

each step
you calculated to perfection

you were the king,
and i,
the queen

the game was fun
for a time

until i began to win

you hated losing

but you made one fateful error

you forgot:
the queen can move anywhere
while you could only move
one space
at a time

did you ever really love me?

or was i just another toy in your

kingdom of terror?

ASH

do you know how much it hurts to look back and realize:

i trusted you with the deepest part of my heart
        and still
                you hungered for my soul
                    so that you could use it
                        to fill the emptiness in yours

                    and the saddest part?

                    i still love you

ASH

you tasted like sugar to my soul
sweet at first taste
and oh so addictive

over-consumption of your love
left me ill

ASH

do i ever creep into your mind
with whispers of love?

do i ever draw you in
with my siren song?

do i ever confess my love
with memories of yesterday?

-   *i hope that even my pretend existence
    is smarter than that*

ASH

she fleetingly wonders how it is possible to feel so
distantly heartbroken
like an observer,
seeing but unfeeling
she thinks she should feel like crying
but she doesn't

maybe some pain is too deep for tears

ASH

the weight of loneliness grows greater with each death

people she never knew
and never would
gone with the vengeance
of an incurable disease

in this world of terrifying unknowns,
she longs for strangers
who could have been friends

- *pandemic*

ASH

i can still see you, sometimes
feel the way you towered over me

your eyes saying run
while your voice pled stay

when you told me of your struggles
perhaps it wasn't an attempt at humility

but rather,
a warning

-    *you used me*

ASH

just another girl trying to stay

afloat

in a sea of conflicting advice

ASH

more memories haunt her (2)

she lies in the dark, looking up

face above her,
saying words she doesn't understand.

she only knows a few:
tomorrow they come

they'll come and they'll take and they'll change it

moving,
leaving home and familiar

she thinks she's excited

she looks up at the face of the one she trusts,
and she wonders

tomorrow, he says
tomorrow the movers are coming

tomorrow means change
tomorrow means uncertainty to a little girl's heart

four years old,
looking up

tomorrow, she thinks

ASH

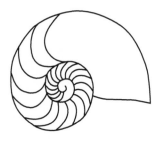

the pieces of his love were like sand
countless
but easily washed away

if nothing else,

you made me learn

ASH

the lonely creeps into her heart and mind,
mocking her

the old feeling permeates her soul,
laughing at the girl she once was,
while whispering that it's all her fault now

if she is all she thought and her loved ones said, *why?*

why this lonely girl, cut off from their understanding
because she lived with a monster?

*why does one person's choices
still dictate the rest of hers?*

ASH

she fears trusting him

one mis-spoken word
and he will be gone

-    TRAUMA

ASH

some nights
she is just a little too tired
and life is just a little too big

-    *quiet*

ASH

she realizes that perhaps
she does not fear the dark as much,
anymore

but she does fear emotion

-     too strong to crack

ASH

numbness sets in
i don't want to withdraw from him

oh darling,
you already have

you so carefully guard your heart
but
you finally decided to let someone in

and then,
once again,
realized it was wrong

the walls go back up,
          and she lets love
                              die

ASH

is this the nail in the coffin,
or does the coffin even exist?

-       *things i ask myself when i can't sleep*

ASH

the hell that destroyed her past
is clawing at her future

she is so tired

she almost wants
to let it
win

ASH

so afraid to
fall
that she may never
fly

-    gravity

94

ASH

she positions the stream of hot water
over her heart

maybe she can wash away
the pain

if nothing else,
at least the water
hides her tears

she is so tired of trying to reason and excuse his way into
her life

she is so weary of *helping him fit*

so many jagged edges
push him out of the spot
she prescribed for him
in her heart

ASH

you keep adjusting the rules of how to please you

how to be funny enough,
pretty enough,
good enough

the rules of this game used to be simple:
smile, you smile back

now it has become the game of balance
trying not to trip the wrong switch
or fall on the wrong square

i am tired of being a player in your game
that was never really safe
to begin with

ASH

please

do not keep breaking and re-breaking this heart that fell
for yours

why was i so blind
to the way you dismiss me

you kept scrawling down addendums
to the way i could be fantastic enough
for you

ASH

you think of me as an option,
an idea to toy with,
until something better comes

when it does, you drift away
and then it doesn't work out,
so you run back

at first my heart waited for yours
i waited for you to look over your shoulder,
see me,
notice me standing there and smiling

the smile only dimmed when you looked away from me,
to some other shiny object i couldn't see

i kept bravely smiling,
pushed the corners of my mouth up
with fingernails painted for you

you walked away
but i comforted myself with the fact that
at least you didn't run

i kept smiling

suddenly you stopped,
looked back,
came back

i welcomed you with open arms,
basking in your wide smiles
and friendly greetings
my smile matched yours
as i slipped you in to the comfortable spot
i had created for you in my heart

ASH

*you held my hand
and my heart*

then
before i could blink,
you shrugged off my hold
and started to jog away

my smile trembled,
but i comforted myself:
at least you didn't run

just before i gave up,
you began to amble back

i forced a happy smile to my face
and listened to my heart,
telling me to go to you

i ignored the niggling *why*
and the humiliation of insecurity

*it'll be alright -
he loves me*

you came back
and slowly,
i let myself smile in full

one day,
i scooped up my shrinking courage
and asked you:
why?

you sent back words
that bit into me
and wounds began to form

ASH

as you walked away,
i replaced my smile with strength
i will still smile at you,
but this time,
my smile is for me
not to please you

your casual implications
that i wasn't quite good enough
to hold your eyes
are finally
enough
to
make
me
run
away

i comfort myself
that i'm not waiting
to be comforted
by you
anymore

ASH

i am not damaged
just wounded

i am not broken
just bruised

i am not messed up
just afraid

she tells herself these things;
it feels less scary if she lies

ASH

eventually,

the pain dies

and she is just left

with scars

ASH

she tastes the sulfur on her tongue
as she struggles to remember something
other than this pain

she was burned alive
and now all that is left
is ash

ASH

you demanded glory
but all my battered heart had left to give
was love

-   *never enough*

ASH

i am not just your toy for entertainment
a reliever for boredom
or a trophy for your possession

-     anymore

ASH

who were you,
before him?

the saddest words she ever spoke:

i don't remember

your eyes mirror the

broken parts of my soul

ASH

he tells her
that he is not afraid
of her tears

don't you see?
it is not you that i am afraid of
i am afraid that i will become more of the me
that used to exist

that once the tears start,
they will not stop

i am afraid
that you will see my tears,
tell me you love me,
and then leave

- *too broken to love?*

ASH

the loneliest nights are when she remembers old pain

ASH

yet more memories haunt her (3)

she feels in her
a loneliness

this is a familiar companion,
yet she pushes it away
will not name one of her greatest fears
of being alone

she stands on the outside
their circle formed
laughter and backstabbing

all she sees
is community
and belonging

she turns away
heat filling her face

don't let them see

weary,
deep down
hiding the broken pieces beneath

she stands outside the circle
and pretends the words
don't cut her heart

peeling back the confidence
she might one day have,
she laughs it off
hiding the tears and scream inside
behind the falseness of belonging

ASH

if she doesn't speak
they won't know

even standing in the circle,
she is distinctly alone

later,
she drives home
with the windows down,
staring at the dim sky

here she is truly alone
but at least she is safe

the scream inside
can be released into the silence

if only she could say to them:
please don't turn away
when someone else catches your eye
don't cast me off

i promise,
i have value too

staring at a screen
and wishing words would appear,
she wonders how long
the lonely
will last

ASH

i am a broken girl
please don't hurt me any more than i already have been
i know how to pick up the pieces
and walk away

but

i am tired

ASH

unwaveringly kind to her

but will it last?

- *what she wonders, sometimes*

ASH

she knows someday she will face it all
but today
is not that day

she's afraid that if she looked pain in the eye,
it would break her

she's not ready to be broken again

how long will it take me to see you

as you

and not him?

-   *mask*

ASH

she woke up crying
dregs of sleep coiled
tightly around her heart
as she remembered

- *ache*

ASH

a few hours of silence
without your voice in my head

that was all i wanted

ASH

your love was a tattoo

painful

and not easily removed

he asked to see her heart
but there are parts of her
that may be too broken
even for him

- *hidden*

ASH

there is a quiet urgency in a girl who says so little
yet does so much

her life is pulsing away
and she is barely hanging on

ASH

her footsteps echo as she walks through
the ghost town of her life

the empty houses
follow her with hollow stares

so much loss
so much pain

each footstep
another rhythm of lonely

there is darkness here

but she vows:
she will find the light

ASH

you walked away from me
and now,
finally,
you run back,
as you realize what you lost

but it's too late, love

the girl you knew

is dead

ASH

if only they knew
how many poems were written
about them

wrung-out, weary words
hopeless and hopeful

if only they knew
that they were the cause
of so much pain

if only they knew
how much i wanted
to save them

maybe they would have listened

ASH

her choice is simple:
choose him or don't
so when did things become so grey?

ASH

she never really learned how to say goodbye
        left her home without a look back

she learned how to say *enough*
        how to walk away after they left,
                but *goodbyes* die on her tongue
                like melting ice

a broken part of her still longs
        to walk back in time
                and say
                        "hello. i'm home."

ASH

she wants to tell them,
wants them to say she is strong too

she's a private soul,
but her fear is more than that

her fear is the danger that would come
if she spoke her secret,
gave voice to the twisted story
that chains her soul

then watched it take on a life of its own

- *monster*

ASH

i see you,
standing there alone

you smile and play with your hair
cough and glance at the ground

i see you,
standing there alone

outcast

i see you standing there
and i remember
                    me

ASH

your romance was like a bomb
exploding with all the things i wanted to hear

i wish i had known then
that your war tactics
were lies

-   *love bomber*

PHOENIX

PHOENIX

she was born
from the ashes
blood tracing her arms
as she grasped the flames
that tried to burn her
and used them to create
new flesh

she rises,
alive

-    phoenix

PHOENIX

she has lived in the cocoon of pretend safety for too long

it's dark in here
but it's known

it hurts to poke at the shield
to press the woven cage

but maybe it would hurt more to remain

her wings are oh so fragile
made of the smallest fibres of hope
that they tried to kill

it breaks her to stretch
but it broke her more to stay

she doesn't look back
as she flies away

- *rebirth*

PHOENIX

i am using the rocks
from your cold heart
to build the foundation
of a new home

*this is a safe place
where you will never be*

PHOENIX

there are

      so
        many
           parts
              to
                 me

they get mixed up sometimes

PHOENIX

you held my hand as i waded into the lava of healing

when the heat began to set your skin on fire,
you walked away
swearing forever love and a bucket of water to cool my
burns

you never returned
but as i was set on fire
i began to live

love,
i understand

PHOENIX

she wishes the hard was not alive and devouring and real

despite understanding it,
she still wants to run away

into that beautiful,
maybe imaginary,
life called *Normal*

PHOENIX

it is okay
to cry
for a man
who never knew
how to love you

you,
in all your
wild
beautiful
pieces

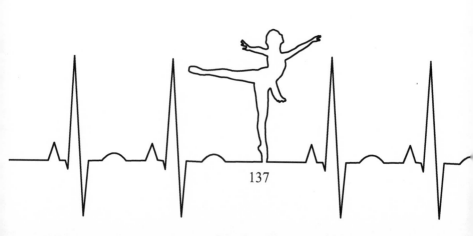

137

PHOENIX

bits of memories
random moments
fear
and emotionless
life

it is as though
her brain is beginning
to try

she doesn't know whether to injure it again
or let it heal

      -    this time, for good

PHOENIX

i will hold your pain

even if my hands shake

PHOENIX

maybe love is giving someone the power
to destroy you
as you share the truth
of yourself

and trusting them not to

PHOENIX

sunsets and embers of a roaring fire

remind me of how brilliantly our love

died

and how beautifully i survived

PHOENIX

the last tendrils of string binding her heart to his
disintegrated

she is no longer holding out hope for a someday

she is moving on from a chapter of a book that was
sketched in running-dry ink

walking away from someone who walked away first

and letting go of someone that she was never meant to
hold

-   *freedom*

PHOENIX

memories are woven into

my burned skin

like beautiful scars

PHOENIX

let your heart rest
it works so hard to protect you
even when it is breaking

PHOENIX

he didn't realize that he was trying
to down a warrior

warriors never go down without a fight
and a scream for their lives
and the ones they love

she was never going to be easy to end

PHOENIX

we exploded

but oh,
we made a beautiful disaster

PHOENIX

don't come too close
i might see rejection on your face

don't walk towards me
you may break on the glass scattered around me

don't touch me
i will burn your fingers

but please
love me

PHOENIX

i have never spoken to you
and likely never will
but i wanted to thank you

your kindness made me believe in the goodness of
humanity again

- stranger

PHOENIX

she breathes in hope,
siphoning out the poisoned air around her

PHOENIX

i blocked you out of my life
without remorse
without feeling

you tried to break my heart
with your game

and finally
i moved my heart away

- *checkmate*

PHOENIX

please keep telling me that i am worth it
until logic
becomes heart

PHOENIX

she releases her old dreams like balloons,
each one sailing away
as her heart finally lets go

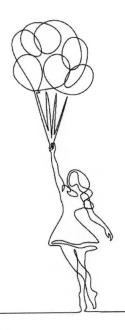

she will replace this pain
with ferocious hope

PHOENIX

she hears her heartbeat

steadying her soul

she is still alive

and

breathing

PHOENIX

what a story this would make someday

- you and me

PHOENIX

i am difficult to win over

my heart is guarded by walls,
and guns,
and pain
that have been put in place by me,
by past romances,
by him

maybe i am hard to love, even

but show me your heart,
your consistency,
your true, honest love,
and you will glimpse me

me, walls down
me, heart trusting
me, soul-deep afraid of telling my guard to rest,
but doing so,
for you

- *easy to love, if you are brave*

PHOENIX

i am like a bomb,
poised to detonate

i paste on a smile,
and somehow
you do not run
from past shrapnel

PHOENIX

she realizes that getting to that place called Free
is never easy

*but tasting the light will be worth the pain
of swallowing the fire*

PHOENIX

i am a hopeless romantic,
a jaded cynic,
a crushed realist.

~~the only thing i am not is too much.~~

want to try your luck at winning my heart?

- *complicated*

PHOENIX

i trace his face with bloodied fingertips
"you are so beautiful, love"
i whisper the words as my hands fall
"but he made me bleed"

it is his turn
i feel his fingers on my scarred skin
"he made you bleed, darling,
but i am here to show you that
you can
heal"

PHOENIX

i am broken

i have seen the darkness
and i have felt the light

i have walked through madness
and i have struggled in sadness

they say you can't be invincible
but i won't let them see me fall

my armour is starting to crack
but i fill in the chips

don't let them see
bar the door
fake it
peace starts with a smile
you are stronger than this

so many things
ring inside my head

but then
an offer
of trust
of letting the pain fall
of having a moment where i do not have to be strong

one tear
and then more

perhaps this is not weakness
like i was told

perhaps it is not weak
to trust

PHOENIX

perhaps it is not weak
to be real
to embrace this strange, painful thing
that ultimately
will heal

i walk through the hard
sometimes crawling
yet a little stronger, now

i will not let this pain break me
or remake me
into something that i am not

i will not lose that sense of beauty
or that joy in loving the world

i will not let the broken break the healed

i can feel the fear
bubbling up inside of me like acid
tearing away at the tender skin
and eating away my bones

i can feel the longing to be away
but
i will still rise

PHOENIX

if you try to keep me down
i will only fly higher

after all,
a phoenix cannot be caged

PHOENIX

her heart was covered in snow
frozen to the ground
buried in the ice that the past created

so safe,
but so cold

he brought an ice pick
and chopped away at the frozen shield

the metal created cuts on her flesh
but as the wounds grew
so did her breathing

his love made her heart melt

164

PHOENIX

you died before my eyes
the kindness that i fell so
desperately
in love with
went up in the most brilliant of flames

i watched you die
as another replaced you
i no longer recognized your face

and i wondered why the flames didn't rebirth you
like they did me

perhaps pain only heals some

PHOENIX

i am proud of these scars,
testaments to each battle fought

i did not win every step
but i won the war

PHOENIX

she recognizes this feeling
familiar, familiar stupidity
the feeling of not being enough-ness

it is a familiar old companion
perhaps she should love the wrinkled leather face of this
timeworn alias,
the disguise of pain

but she loathes the moment
when it will show up
knocking at the doors of her mind and heart,
beating down the resolve that tries to wrap itself around
her in a protective layer

her fighter resolve doesn't usually win
it doesn't tonight, but maybe she can force the leather
straps down and around the wriggling, shaking mass that
she calls Heart

goodbye, fear
goodnight
i need to sleep now
go to sleep, insecurities
leave me for another eight hours
banish yourself until the daylight hours
when you will return and i will struggle with you again and
i will hold this burden and wish wish wish that i could
drop it

she fears that eventually her hands will break

she wants to live fully alive
happy
not holding this raging mass in her two bloodied and
bruised hands

167

PHOENIX

they deserve to rest
she deserves to rest

the day that her hands begin to crack,
bone peeking through the peeling skin,
she lays down the familiar old frame
of insecurity
and walks away

PHOENIX

part of her longs to go back to yesterday

yesterday, when the world was alive and she breathed in
hope
yesterday, when her future seemed steady
yesterday, when she didn't know what she knows today

but

if she returned to yesterday she would never have
tomorrow
and the past would mark her forever

she realizes;
she would rather claim the pain and bits of beauty of this
present moment
than seal herself off from the joy of that sunshine-dipped
word:

tomorrow

maybe her wounds can help heal their's

PHOENIX

broken

her fingernails pick at the scab of her past,
pulling away shards of blackened flesh

she draws the word *broken* in blood,
accepting her fate

underneath the blood,
there is new life,
struggling to grow from the crusty remains

she longs to survive the pain one last time
but she also wants to live

she knows she has to shatter to become whole

she dreads it
but she would rather be broken in strength
by her own choice
than remain broken by a hand not her own

this is healing

darling,
don't break everything that's beautiful within you
simply because the world said it wasn't

PHOENIX

love does not mean sacrificing yourself on the altar of
someone else's existence

- *she is learning*

PHOENIX

don't play with fire, she whispered
but then fire played with her

so she became the fire

PHOENIX

i stitched my broken skin together
with strands of gold
formed from the pieces i mined

your lust for gold and jewels
will not win this time

i am becoming a new thing
and you will never touch me again

i tattooed hope on my ribs

and courage in my soul

PHOENIX

i can never forget you
but i will heal

      -    *without you*

PHOENIX

i miss you
but i have to believe
that you are not
the only
one
who could love
the broken mess
called
me

PHOENIX

things i'll never tell you

i never told you, because i wanted to move on
i wanted to breath without the memory of you

you hurt me
with your words of care and then your actions that proved
them false

still, i long for you to reach out
if you did, i would tell you the words i never will:

i don't feel like i know you
anymore
not the way i thought i did

you treated me as expendable
not worth your effort

you were what i wanted but
now i have new dreams

what i'd tell you
but never will?

goodbye

PHOENIX

promises
some broken, some kept

the ones that hurt
that stole
those are the ones she has to
let go of

i promise it will never end:
a life that disappeared

i promise i'm safe:
a man who broke her

i promise i love you:
a person who refused

i promise i'll stay:
a girl who didn't

i promise it will be ok:
it wasn't

so today
she lays down the promises
the broken dreams
the fractured hopes

and promises
herself
that she will heal

PHOENIX

her soul has begun to sing again

after so many years of silence

PHOENIX

she is beginning to rise

her paper wings
        set on fire as she flies
                too close to the sun

but she does not fly away
        for she knows
                as a phoenix
                        she must die

                            to live

PHOENIX

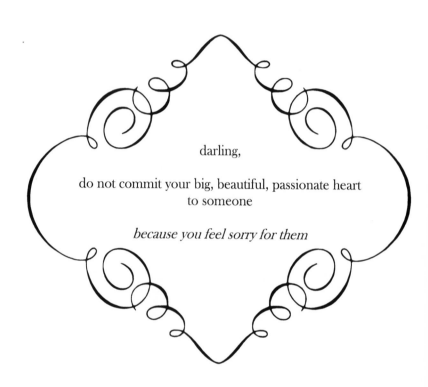

darling,

do not commit your big, beautiful, passionate heart
to someone

because you feel sorry for them

PHOENIX

each day,
i am discovering more parts of me that disappeared for
you

i love them

PHOENIX

burning ink

you will not read this letter

it will go in the box
that i keep beneath my bed

it will stay with your other words,
hidden poems of the dreams we would be

someday,
you will burn the letters
i wrote to you
so that you can forget the loss

i will burn yours too

you and i,
we will be connected once again
in a brief moment of time

each holding the words of the right one,
our person

we will inhale,
you and i,
and then carefully burn away
the whispered dreams of yesterday
until there is nothing left
but ash

perhaps you will mourn the loss;
i may be broken,
but i am not forgettable
yes,
perhaps you will feel sorrow
as our paths depart in this final step

PHOENIX

me?
i will hold that last letter,
the one you wrote to me
before we exploded
like stars in the galaxy

i will linger over the words
and wonder if we could have made it

and then i will burn
your final words to me,
inhale,
and walk into
tomorrow

PHOENIX

she learned how to blend in so well
invisibility was her friend

smile and be quiet and pretend that stifling her voice was
fun
pretend that this was her

she learned how to play the part they wanted
sometimes she was good at it
sometimes she fell short

now
every day
she is becoming more of her

a girl made of fire can't blend in

PHOENIX

my heart is finished with you

i wavered every time i saw you
and now
i am settled

i loved the parts of you that never existed

you do not want me
and i have decided
that i do not want you

\-   *you taught me how to say goodbye*

188

PHOENIX

part I

i am dancing alone,
missing the magic of our childhood
when we believed in each other
and the beauty of life

do you ever think of me?

PHOENIX

part II

i missed you

three simple words
that make my heart
gasp for breath

i missed you too

PHOENIX

i am madly in love with the person i am becoming

-     self love

PHOENIX

free spirit,
they called her

she loved to fly
because she knew what it felt like
to fall

PHOENIX

becoming is never easy

it means leaving behind everything that does not let your
spirit soar

it means abandoning the past that captured your heart in
its chains

it means *freedom*

PHOENIX

you promised me a forever love
if only i could stand a little pain

but love,
forever does not require wounds

i see the strength in your eyes

i promise:

you will survive

L
I
G
H
T

LIGHT

sunshine dreams rise
    as she dips her toes
        in the clear waters
           of a new life

LIGHT

the broken girl
hands the boy the knife
either she makes him bleed with her pain
or she frees him
and slaughters herself

the boy takes the knife
lays it down
takes her hand
and they walk away

let me love you

i used to dream
that i could soar
into outer space
on my little swing set

i was never very good
at keeping my feet
on the ground

- dreamer

LIGHT

he asked her why she loves poetry

she smiled

because poetry is like music

it makes me *feel*

LIGHT

i'm proud of you

i'm proud of you
for getting up
when humanity was pushing you down

i'm proud of you
for saying something
when silence was the only question

i'm proud of you
for using what burned you
to create a wildfire of hope

i'm proud of you
for overcoming a love
so strong
that it could not be broken
only twisted

i'm proud of you
for still standing
and shining
when your world was buried alive

if you have not heard it yet:
you deserve to be proud,
too

LIGHT

after all you've been through,
you deserve the best this broken earth
can carry

wait for a man who will treat you like gold

LIGHT

your touch heals the broken pieces of me
your voice soothes the frantic pace of my heart

and finally,
the mask of projection,
of believing you to be like him
slips away

i just see you

LIGHT

seek me at the edge of hope

standing with a handful of rope

find me,

grasping light 'til the end

i will meet you there

LIGHT

she traces her scars,

the roadmap of her heart's broken journey.

she wears these scars now with a smile.

"see?" she whispers. "i survived."

-   *and so will you*

you hold the map to all the worlds
i want to explore

-   with you

LIGHT

i will never trap you

your heart screams for freedom
while your mind longs for safety

i want to love you the way you deserve

those men in the past were boys
seeing a body
instead of the soul in your eyes

you covered up for them
laughed for them
complimented and acted and smiled for them

i am here to be different

i see your heart,
afraid of trust
and of breaking mine

this heart of mine can take it
if only to get the chance to love yours

don't you see who you are?
you are so much more than your body
your eyes
your skin

i see you
for who you are
and i
love
you

LIGHT

the girl with the broken smile
see her
see the light in her eyes?

love her well,
for that light can become a fire

treat her with tenderness
but also equality
strength
and respect

for she was not broken because she was weak

LIGHT

do not come to rescue me from my tower.
i don't need to be rescued;
i have already saved myself

but if you want to run alongside me and into the
adventure then:
let's run

her fear speaks
but her hope triumphs

LIGHT

you are not alone, love
sometimes it takes a lot of darkness
to see

-    light

LIGHT

thank you for not making me
feel as though i have to hide myself
to be loved by you

       -    *seen*

LIGHT

your courage makes you so beautiful

LIGHT

maybe today,
in all it's broken beauty,
is exactly
where you are meant to be

-    letter to me

LIGHT

darling,
in the midst of this beautiful life, remember:
do not lose yourself to find others

she leans down

to let her whispered breath

give life to the ghosts of dreams

LIGHT

your dreams are beginning

to see the light

it's time to let them breathe

LIGHT

darling,
wild girl,

wait for a man who will jump in puddles beside you
hold your hand beneath the stars
dream with you
laugh with you

and wade into the waters of pain while holding you on his
shoulders

wait for tenderness

LIGHT

girl of stardust,
it is time to shine His light
into the endless night

LIGHT

she's just a girl with a million pictures,

dreams bigger than can fit on paper,

starlight in her heart despite the darkness,

a song on her lips,

hair that refuses to stay tamed,

a spirit of adventure and wildness and freedom that at
times

overwhelms her

a dreamer mind,

a musical performer and listener and lover

the girl who dances in the kitchen and sings off-key

the girl who will smile even when it's raining

and the girl with a spirit that dreams of wandering beyond,

past the limits and past the sky

- just a girl

LIGHT

someday i will tell my daughter

of her worth

and how precious her bright,
beautiful soul is

i will tell her these things
so that she will never have to seek them
from someone else

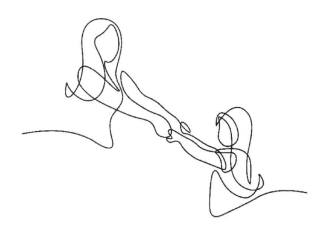

LIGHT

life is too short to twist who you are to fit the mold Life
says you must live in

maybe your whole beautiful self wasn't made for a mold

LIGHT

i'm not here to control you
i'm only here to discover,
to love,
to stand in your storms
and hold your hand in the battle

-    *side by side*

wait for a love
soaked in the beauty
of honesty and laughter

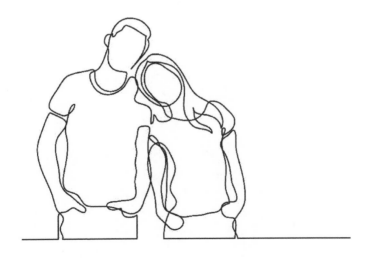

a galaxy of stars

could not compare

to the light in your eyes

LIGHT

i dance beneath the light of the stars
as i learn to sing without you

LIGHT

there is stardust in my pulsing veins

you don't own this fire anymore

LIGHT

i've always kinda craved adventure

do you want to be my forever adventure?

she touched his face.

"i am afraid to love you."

he smiled.

"i know.

but
i will stay
and i will love you

until you are no longer afraid."

LIGHT

a lifelong love

she holds his hand
you are mine
as the years go by

quiet whispers
i still see you
even as her eyes begin to fade

holding close
i am still here
as the years go by

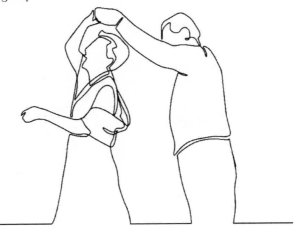

LIGHT

i fell for you

now i am falling for the love of life
the wind
the stars
the puddle jumping
the people
and the beauty of living

i am in love with the breath in my lungs

LIGHT

a girl of stardust and gold,

she breathes freedom

and beautiful dreams

LIGHT

she holds entire worlds of hope
in her gentle hands

LIGHT

they all say to wait for love that is magical
that is passionate
that is easy

perhaps we would all be happier
if we waited for love
that was safe

LIGHT

my scars breathe no shame
for my wings are growing
from the wounds you left

LIGHT

i will love you

and when you are afraid

i will love you even more

because i see the beauty in your scars

LIGHT

years later
    she sucks in a breath at the surface
        then dives again beneath the waves
          that tried to drown her
         to save those
          still left below

LIGHT

born of fire
living in the aftermath of ash
rising as a phoenix

and now,
dancing in the light

armor – part II

trauma feels like too-tight armor that someone has forced on you and then wrapped with chains and a lock.

the armor protects you from the bad, but also from the good. it doesn't let anyone past. it guards your heart and your body from experiencing anything it doesn't want to. it finally has control. *you* finally have control, a grasp on a reality that was so chaotic.

it feels safe, for the first time that you can remember. it is lonely in there, but it is safety when you had none.

it is too tight, but you learn to breathe. sometimes you almost forget it is there. you learn to breathe, and then laugh, and run. you are so close to being that person who used to live in all that light and trust before your world exploded; now you just have a bit of extra weight to carry around.

you can't unlock the armor. even when you almost forget, you always know it is there, weighing you down until you feel like you will sink into the ground. sometimes you pick at the lock, but it makes your fingers bleed and the metal dig into your chest. it hurts far more to remember, and try to get free, when you already know how to breathe and live with it.

you want love, and some try to get past the armor. a few brave souls make it past the outer layer, but they can never quite reach your heart because the armor is tight, protecting you. you show them the personality and spirit that has survived the armor, but the wounds are hidden. safe.

LIGHT

the only way to get free is to cut the lock, because the person who created the key to freedom destroyed it, and then you.

cutting the lock means pain. oh so much pain, and remembering, and reopening the scars that hide beneath the armor. the scars still feel fresh, sometimes. they are always there. you don't want to cry anymore.

cutting the lock means feeling helpless again. powerless. it means giving up the protection of the armor. feeling – and being – helpless is your greatest fear. you long to be protected, and the cold metal guarding your heart feels safe.

yet only when the armor is gone can you live fully alive.

your fingers are bleeding and your heart is wounded, but you want to try.

trying feelings far scarier than living the way you always have, but maybe,

on the other side,

there is hope.

LIGHT

a dreamer,
a wild rebel girl

she dances in sunlight
and lives in the stars

LIGHT

dreaming with eyes open
and full of stars

-    *forever*

ACKNOWLEDGEMENTS

To A, my incredible mama and the one person who never gave up on me. Thank you for showing me light when I only saw ashes, and encouraging me all throughout my life to write.

To my beautiful ones, my family, who have walked with me through every step of this journey and are the most amazing people I know.

To B, who has shown me endless kindness and been my partner-in-crime [legal, not-crime ;)] so many times.

To S, who gave me the tools to heal and the time I needed to take them.

To C & M, who have shown me so much love and amazing care.

To all of my incredible friends and family, who have walked with me through the ups and downs of this beautiful life.

To the exceptionally talented creators at Sam & Wren – thank you for providing so much feedback and help with designing this book! Your work is unparalleled.

To my incredible advance readers – thank you all from the bottom of my heart for taking a chance on my debut collection. Your encouragement and support means the world to me.

To the Phoenix Risers launch team - you are all amazing, and I am so thankful for each of you and your incredible help in getting Tears of Ash and Light into the world and the hands of readers.

To all of the fantastic writers and friends I have connected with on social media (Instagram in particular). There are too many of you to name, but each of you are so special to me. Thank you for everything, from genuine connection to sharing & supporting my work.

To Connilyn Cossette - when I emailed you as a young teen author all those years ago to ask for an endorsement for a novel, you gave the encouragement that kept me going. You also told me to keep writing... and I did. Thank you for seeing me.

To my readers, who gave these words a home and listened to my story. Thank you.

And most of all, to my Lord and Savior, Jesus Christ, who made all of this possible while creating beauty from ashes. You are my Everything.

ABOUT

Purple Phoenix Poetry was born out of the ashes of a life that became light.

I write to share hope in the darkness and take you on a journey of self-discovery, grasping light, and finding love in the broken mosaic of life.

dreaming with eyes open and full of stars

Made in the USA
Columbia, SC
10 April 2021